```
D0340210
```

TopGear

HOW TO

PARACHUTE
INTO A MOVING CAR

13 5 7 9 10 8 6 4 2

Published in 2013 by BBC Books, an imprint of Ebury Publishing.
A Random House Group Company.

Text © Richard Porter 2013
Illustrations © The Comic Stripper 2013

Top Gear (word marks and logos) is a trademark of the
British Broadcasting Corporation and used under licence. Top Gear © 2005

The Random House Group Limited Reg. No. 954009

Addresses for companies within the Random House Group
can be found at www.randomhouse.co.uk

A CIP catalogue record for this book is available from the British Library.

ISBN: 978 1 849 90635 7

The Random House Group Limited supports the Forest Stewardship Council® (FSC®),
the leading international forest-certification organisation. Our books carrying the
FSC label are printed on FSC®-certified paper. FSC is the only forest-certification
scheme supported by the leading environmental organisations, including Greenpeace. Our
paper procurement policy can be found at www.randomhouse.co.uk/environment

Commissioning editor: Lorna Russell
Project editor: Joe Cottington
Copy editor: Ian Gittins
Design: Amazing15
Illustrations: The Comic Stripper
Production: Antony Heller

Colour origination by Amazing15
Printed and bound in Germany by
Firmengruppe APPL, aprinta druck, Wemding, Germany

To buy books by your favourite authors and register for
offers visit www.randomhouse.co.uk

TopGear

HOW TO

PARACHUTE
INTO A MOVING CAR

VITAL SURVIVAL TIPS
FOR THE MODERN MAN

RICHARD PORTER

BBC
BOOKS

CONTENTS >>>

The modern world is full of tricky challenges and tiresome obstacles. From buying trousers and making a sandwich to receiving directions and building an amphibious car, there are so many things that require a chap to show expertise; yet knowing instinctively how to tackle every potential problem or puzzle is impossible. After all, the memory is finite, and there's always the risk that learning in detail how to design a Pagani Zonda or play rugby with cars will overwrite some other vital skill, such as how to drive or use a revolving door properly.

Thankfully, that's no longer a concern thanks to the very book you hold before you now. Within these pages you will find handy guides and hints applicable to literally any situation the world can throw at you. Think of it as an instruction manual for life. Except that, unlike an actual instruction manual, you should probably read this rather than glancing disdainfully at the cover and then shoving it in a kitchen drawer where it will be impossible to find at that crucial moment when all the alarms are going off, several lights are flashing and there is a smell of hot plastic that you really wish would go away.

How to Parachute into a Moving Car really is all the book you will ever need. Especially if you want to parachute into a moving car.

DISCLAIMER
Warning: most of the advice in this book is idiotic and should be ignored.

It's now even easier to gauge the difficulty of everyday tasks with our handy **How Hard Can it Be?-o-meter!**

HOW HARD CAN IT BE?

0   5   10

HOW TO... ⟩⟩⟩

...BUY PETROL

1. Find a free pump. Pull up. Put the correct nozzle into your car.

2. Adopt your chosen petrol-station stance (see pages 12–15).

3. Wonder why all petrol pumps appear to have a dicky prostate and dispense fuel in a sort of listless drizzle that makes filling up an average car feel like it takes seven hours.

4. Go to the petrol-station shop and pay for your fuel. Probably buy a bag of Haribo while you're there, not because you need them but because they are on offer, even though you know they're *always* on offer, unlike your dentist, who never seems to do 'offers'.

5. Return to your car. Now here's the VERY important bit. Get into the car, start the engine, put on your seat belt, put it in gear and drive away.

6. Let's just repeat that to make it quite clear: in car, engine on, belt on, in gear, away. There's probably someone else waiting to use that pump and, who knows, they might even be in a hurry. They will thank you for your prompt departure from the forecourt.

7. What you must NOT do is get back into your car and decide that this is the moment to rummage around in your bag for 20 minutes or re-programme all of your radio station pre-sets or get to work on that six-part novel you've been meaning to write. Basically, anything that prevents you from moving off like a scalded F1 driver 2 seconds after getting into your car is wrong.

8. Just to reiterate: in, start, belt, gear, go. And when Jeremy comes to power, those who fail to follow this simple routine will feel the punishing power of his petrol-station-mounted machine-gun nests.

...FIND YOUR PETROL-STATION STANCE

Filling up with petrol is, as we know, an extremely tedious process, especially if you've just had to wait 20 minutes for another motorist to finish reading an entire sodding magazine before moving away (as we have just covered). However, one of the worst parts of filling up is trying to find the right stance to adopt for maximum comfort as you wait for the pump to slowly drizzle droplets of fuel into your tank. Here are a few suggestions.

1. **The car-facing stand**
    Simple, classic, uncomplicated. On the downside, you risk neck-ache from turning your head to see the pump read-out and it does leave you with a 'spare arm' hanging limply by your side.

2. **The car-facing stand (with other hand in pocket)**
    Solves the 'spare arm' problem of the

above but can look slovenly, especially at
more formal petrol stations.

3. **The car-facing lean**
Solves the 'spare arm' problem by
putting that arm to work, leaning on the
roof of the car. Simple, stylish, effective.
Can make you look a bit like a rubbish
catalogue model, though, and not much
use with very low or very high cars
unless you want to sprain something.

4. **The reverse lean**
Once the nozzle is in the side of the car,
turn around and rest your arse and your
'spare arm' on the side of the car, using
a backhand grip on the pump trigger.
Relaxed, stylish and gives an excellent
view of the pump read-out.

5. **The sitting inside the car where it's nice
and warm**
Hang on a minute, you might be thinking,
how can you do that? Well, you can do
it if you go to certain other countries
such as the United States, where the
petrol pumps have a latch that lets you
set them going and then walk away to
pursue other interests for 5 minutes.
Gosh, you might exclaim, that sounds

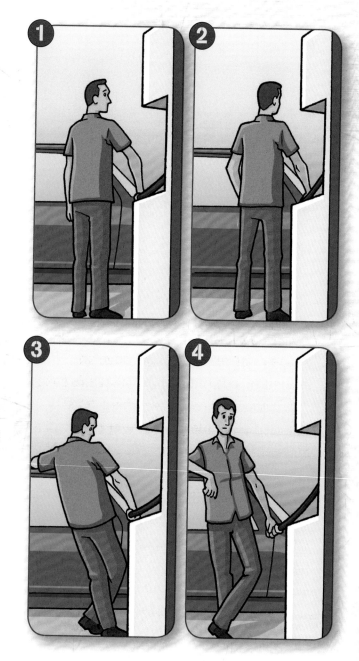

dangerous! Yet the pumps have an automatic cut-out and, for heaven's sake, they allow it in America, where, let's not forget, people get sued for selling coffee that's too hot. So Americans can enjoy this luxury while the poor British motorist has to stand in a blizzard to take care of their fuel needs AND pays a great deal more for the privilege. Why, cruel oil companies, WHY?

...FIND YOUR CAR IN A CAR PARK

We've all been there. Whether it's at a theme park or an out-of-town shopping-cinema-and-misery complex, you park for an hour or two and then can't quite remember exactly where. How best to hunt down your car and get the flipping heck out of there? Here are a few tips.

1. Carry a step-ladder in the car and take it with you when you park. Upon your return to the parking area, simply erect the ladder and use it as an elevated vantage point from which to find your car.

2. When you park, leave a large and heavy object such as a chest of drawers or anvil leaning against the steering wheel, thereby activating your car's horn. When you return to the car park, simply head towards the constant and annoying noise.

3. Not in a hurry? Simply wait until the shopping centre or amusement park has closed and everyone else has gone home. Hey presto, by a process of elimination,

your car must be the one that's left!

4. When leaving your car, set it on fire. Upon your return to the car park, the thick column of black smoke, lethal 10-foot-tall tongues of flame, wildly panicking shoppers and attending trio of fire engines will guide you immediately back to where you started!

5. Install Jeremy Clarkson and Richard Hammond's unique Old Person's Car Locator System™ comprising the 'long-range' rocket-propelled flares and the 'short-range' bright orange, helium-filled weather balloon. All your car-finding needs in one handy, remotely operated package. Warning: does NOT work well in multi-storey car parks, and may cause a bit of a scene.

HOW **HARD** CAN IT **BE?**

0   5   10

...ANNOY AMERICANS

1. First of all, you have to find the right sort of Americans to annoy. People in California are too laid back, and people in New York only get annoyed if you take longer than 2 seconds to give a breakfast order that contains 17 different elements and nine specific instructions. No, to really wind up Americans in the approved *Top Gear* manner you'll need to head to the South, preferably the bit in the bottom-right corner where teeth are a luxury item and 'sister' is a synonym for 'wife'.

2. Buy a crappy old car. Some sort of vast 1970s or 1980s land yacht would be ideal but a murderer's Camaro or a ratty pick-up truck will suffice.

3. Paint your car with slogans. For maximum effect, think what would attract the attention of the average hick, making his moustache bristle and the hairs on the back of his neck stand up (underneath his mullet). Here are some suggestions:

O-BAMA O-K!
OVAL TRACKS IS FOR IDIOTS
GOD ALSO MADE ADAM AND STEVE
WEARIN' VESTS IS FOR HOMOSEXUALS
KENNY ROGERS HAS A SMELLY BEARD

4. Drive about for a bit, perhaps stopping at a gas station until you hear the reassuring sound of rocks raining down on your paintwork and the comforting sight of a pick-up full of rednecks waving guns coming to toast yo' bony ass back to wherever the hell you done be come from.

5. You now have two choices: 1) run away or 2) die. Good luck!

HOW HARD CAN IT BE?

0   5   10

...DRIVE AN AUDI

1. Become a recruitment consultant. Or maybe an estate agent. Either is good. Basically, you just need to work in an industry that attracts terrible human beings, and which the human race has inexplicably allowed to flourish even though, if you think about it, we could manage perfectly well without them.

2. Prepare for the delivery of your new company car by applying another 5 kilos of 'product' to your hair and fitting yourself with one of those headcock Bluetooth in-ear things. Also, go out and buy a massive, chunky watch and a pair of wrap-around sunglasses.

3. Get the keys to your Audi. Go to the nearest motorway and spend all day driving up and down it at a distance of no more than 3mm from the back bumper of the car in front.

4. Completely ignore the fact that everyone else on the road thinks you are a vile,

pushy little twerp, and utterly hates you (apart from BMW drivers, who are just thankful that you've taken the heat off them, at last).

5. Some years later, die alone.

...BE A VICTORIAN EXPLORER

After plunging into the heart of Africa for the 2013 *Top Gear Christmas Special* (that wasn't on at Christmas), Jeremy, Richard and James had a sudden realisation. Being an explorer in Victorian times was bloody brilliant! If you would like to have a crack at it yourself, here's how (but, remember, to really make this work you'll first have to travel back in time to somewhere around 1857).

1. Trouser a whole load of cash from the Royal Geographical Society on the understanding that you are off to explore uncharted parts of Africa.

2. Head off to the great continent and make your way to some bit of the map that looks a bit blank at the moment.

3. Discover that the area you've chosen is rather nice, boasting an agreeable climate, friendly locals, and acres of trees and bushes practically bent double with tasty, succulent fruits. Decide to stay for a while.

4. Send a telegram home telling of great bravery, terrible hardship and 'intense experience of malaria' (failing to add that Malaria is the name of a local girl you've been getting on rather well with). Don't forget to ask for more money.

5. Go for a bit of a stroll. Discover a big waterfall. Name it after yourself.

6. Draw the waterfall and some huts on the map. Pop home, show it to your sponsors in London, trouser another load of cash and repeat as necessary.

HOW HARD CAN IT BE?

0   5   10

HOW TO... >>>

...DRESS LIKE JAMES MAY

1. Find a charity shop that hasn't had any new donations since 1976.

2. Buy all their clothes off them.

...DRIVE A CONVERTIBLE CAR WITH THE ROOF DOWN

(IF YOU ARE UNDER THE AGE OF 30)

1. Put the roof down.

2. Away you go.

...DRIVE A CONVERTIBLE CAR WITH THE ROOF DOWN

(IF YOU ARE OVER THE AGE OF 30)

1. Where no one can see you.

HOW HARD CAN IT BE?

HOW TO... ⟫⟫⟫

...MAKE THE PAGANI ZONDA

1. Come up with the most brilliant, bonkers, exciting and unusual body style you can.

2. Ring Mercedes and ask really, really nicely if you could buy a few of their AMG V12 engines.

3. Make the interior a riot of amazing metal sculpture and mad leather straps.

4. Put your car on sale. Tempt buyers by throwing in a free pair of shoes with every car. Super rich people like it when they get free shoes.

5. Cause Richard Hammond to almost explode with excitement.

6. Give it a few years and then announce that production of your amazing and exciting car must come to an end. That's it. There will be no more.

7. Make one more.

8. That's all, folks. If you wanted a Zonda you're out of luck because they're all gone.

9. Apart from this one you just made.

10. And this one.

11. And these five. But they're just a special edition so that doesn't count.

12. Oh, no! You got to the factory this morning and discovered that in the night someone had broken in and made a Zonda! The swines!

13. Announce the Zonda Final Edition, of which there will be just three made.

14. Plus another one for your friend Eduardo.

15. And that chap you met in an airport.

16. But that really is it. You have stopped making Zondas.

17. Well, one more couldn't hurt now, could it... etc., etc.

HOW HARD CAN IT BE?

0   5   10

...MAKE A CAR FOR OLD PEOPLE

The population of Britain is getting older. Indeed, some researchers think that by 2030 the whole of the country will be old. Apart from young people, who will continue to be young. Some slightly better researchers have discovered that whereas 40 years ago only 15 per cent of people over 70 had a driving licence, it's now almost 60 per cent. Yet at the same time, cars are getting ever more technical and complicated and designed to appeal only to tech-savvy teenagers. Plainly this doesn't make sense, and *Top Gear* decided to do something about it. Perhaps you would like to as well, in which case just follow these handy steps.

Sandwich Fridge

Comfy Chairs

1. Find a suitable car. It must be something

quite tall with big doors so it's easy to get in and out of. It should also have soft suspension for a nice, osteoporosis-friendly ride. Even then you should also consider fitting softer springs. Car-makers these days are obsessed with making everything feel 'sporty', which is basically just another word for 'uncomfortable'.

2. Once you have bought your car, attack the dashboard with a hammer and get rid of all those stupid, confusing switches and buttons. Your car needs just two switches – lights on and off, and wipers

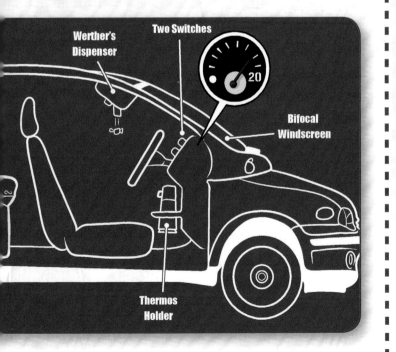

on and off – and two buttons: one to turn the radio on, and one to control the heater temperature, which must be marked 'just right'. You can, if you wish, add a rear fog-light switch since old people seem to find this comforting and like to operate it as soon as there is a light drizzle but, precisely because old people find this comforting and like to operate it as soon as there is a light drizzle, in this case the switch must be connected to precisely nothing.

3. Recalibrate the speedometer so that it runs up to a maximum of 20mph. That way, the old person driving will feel they are keeping to a speed they are happy with, whereas in truth they will be travelling fast enough to avoid causing hold-ups. It's a win-win situation, and the only possible side-effect is that the elderly driver will think roadside trees have got faster these days.

4. Style is important, even for the elderly. That's why you should re-paint your car in a pensioner-friendly colour such as

light beige, dark beige or tartan. A similar philosophy should be applied to the seat fabrics, which should also be waterproof to minimise problems after one of Albert's 'little accidents'.

5. Detail is everything, which is why your car should be fitted with thoughtful touches like a Thermos-flask holder, a Werther's Original dispenser and a special fridge that makes thin, meat-paste sandwiches extra curly at the edges. If you're being really thoughtful, why not install a bi-focal windscreen?

6. You're ready to go. We said, YOU'RE READY TO GO. Yes, READY. TO. GO. Lovely.

...MAKE A HAM SANDWICH

(THE JEREMY CLARKSON WAY)

1. Right, then! First, get some bread. White will do. No mucking about with that stupid eco peace bread that has lentils and mouse droppings in it.

2. Find some ham. From the ham shop.

3. Toasted bread is nicer, so put the bread on the worktop and apply your flamethrower.

4. Oh. The flamethrower appears to have ruined the bread. And the kitchen.

5. Get some more bread. Slap the ham on to it.

6. Shout, 'LUNNNNNNCH!' at extremely high volume for no apparent reason while hitting the bread and ham with a hammer.

7. Oh. That's not gone well.

8. Buy a ham sandwich from a sandwich shop.

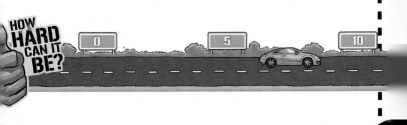

HOW TO... »»

...MAKE A VEGETARIAN MEAL

1. Go to the shop and buy all the ingredients you need. Remember that the main thing about vegetarians is they cannot eat meat. With that in mind, here are the things you must NOT attempt to serve:

Beef
Lamb
Pork
Chicken
Fish, probably

Again, just to reiterate, the main point of vegetarianism is NOT eating the above. In case that isn't clear, here are some of the things a vegetarian house-guest would be happy to eat:

Carrots	Wallpaper
Potatoes	Tyres
Celery	Mud
Moss	Hats
Leaves	Sparrow
Twigs	Lark
Bark	Fox
Rice Krispies	

This is not a comprehensive list. Also, some of the things on it may be worth double-checking with your guest, but you get the idea.

2. Take your ingredients and place them in a bowl. Mix well, stirring in some lukewarm tap water as necessary.

3. Dump the resultant mix on to a plate and garnish with the contents of the little tray thing from the bottom of a well-used hole-punch.

4. Apologise profusely.

5. Suggest going to a restaurant.

HOW
HARD
CAN IT
BE?

0   5   10

...CLIMB A TREE

Being able to climb a tree is a vital skill for any man to have. It can come in handy in a variety of situations, such as cat rescue, ball retrieval and illegal stalking. However, there are many things to consider when attempting to climb a tree. Has it got enough branches to permit adequate hand- and leg-placement? Has it got dense foliage that may impede progress further up the tree? These are all worthy things to worry about, but ultimately irrelevant. You are a man, your tree-climbing endeavours will draw an expectant crowd, and these are the only steps you need to follow:

1. Shout, 'WATCH THIS!'

2. Make frenzied assault on tree, rapidly reaching a height of more than 7 feet.

3. Fall, break arm, go to hospital.

...MAKE AN AMPHIBIOUS CAR

Like jet packs and houses on the moon, amphibious cars are something we've been promised for years, and yet every attempt to make them a commercial reality seems to end in failure. So, if you want a car that's also a boat the only realistic option is to make it yourself, and that's where *Top Gear*'s valuable experience comes in.

1. Do not listen to James May. He will only try to talk you into fitting your car with a sail, which will result in the directional rigour of a house fly and a top speed that's actually a minus number. When it comes to amphibious cars, the man is a shaggy-haired buffoon and has proven this on television. Twice.

2. Do not listen to Richard Hammond either. In fact, *really* don't listen to Richard Hammond. Not unless you want to end your days at the bottom of the sea in a coffin the shape of a Volkswagen camper van. Not that you'll

even make it to the sea because all of Hammond's idiotic designs seem to have an on-road top speed of 3 mph.

3. Oddly enough, for once you might do well to copy the actions of Jeremy Clarkson, because his amphibious car design skills are well-proven and successful. Although when we say 'well-proven' we mean 'capable of working a couple of times' and when we say 'successful' we mean 'no one drowned'.

...MAKE AN AMPHIBIOUS CAR

Even so, it's worth taking Clarkson's infamous Toyboata and Nissank designs as your inspiration. So, basically, buy an old pick-up truck.

4. Don't forget the expanding foam. Lots of expanding foam. Stuff every gap and crevice with the stuff, and when you've got to a point where you think, 'Well that seems to be enough expanding foam' that's actually the point at which you need about twice as much again. Just remember to leave some holes for the engine to breath.

5. Propulsion is a vital matter here, unless you're James May and you're quite happy drifting around in circles getting repeatedly smacked about the head by the boom. What you're going to need is a massive outboard motor. When you go into the shop and ask, in a strident voice, for a massive outboard motor, wait until they show you what they've got and then ask for an even more massive one. That should be massive enough. Unless it makes the back of your pick-up

disappear under the water. Then it might be too massive. Or you haven't fitted enough expanding foam. Probably the second one.

6. Once your amphibious pick-up is finished, take it for a drive. Is there a hot smell? Has some unspecified part inside the dashboard started making an odd buzzing noise? Can you see flames? If you can answer 'no' to all of these, well done. Most importantly, is your vehicle

...MAKE AN AMPHIBIOUS CAR

capable of starting, stopping, going around corners and achieving speeds in excess of 17mph? If you can answer 'yes' then you're well on your way to amphibiousnessnessness.

7. Now for the next major hurdle: you need to go for a practice run on an inland body of water such as a lake or reservoir. Deep breaths, away you go. Oh, wait, you might want to put on a wetsuit first. Probably should have mentioned that earlier.

8. Did you sink? If yes, go back and try again. With about 20 times more expanding foam. If the answer is no, well done. You are ready to go for the big one. A Channel crossing.

9. Don't forget your passport.

Alternatively, did you know they now have car ferries that can cross the English Channel? Just a thought.

HOW TO... »»

...PLAY CAR SAUNA

1. Wait for a nice hot day, preferably when you car has been standing in the sun for a good long time.

2. Assemble one or more friends and invite them to join you in your car.

3. While in traffic, turn the heater on to its highest setting, and the fan to maximum.

4. The first person to open a window or get out of the car is the loser.

5. The point of this game is... er...

...BE A HIGHWAYS AGENCY TRAFFIC OFFICER

1. To start with, it would help if you are the kind of person who wasn't very popular at school and doesn't get invited to things. A slightly angry, bitter sort. Perhaps with a moustache.

2. Spend a week learning how to stack traffic cones.

3. Get the keys to a Day-Glo Mitsubishi Shogun and start driving up and down the motorway at 68mph with a strangely stoical expression on your face, getting a secret thrill from making people slow down, because, from a distance, you look a bit like a policeman (even though the police rejected you at the application stage ten years ago for being too stupid).

4. Notice that the wheel trim from a 1997 Vauxhall Astra has rolled harmlessly into the central reservation.

5. Close the entire motorway for 20 miles in each direction and keep it closed for seven hours so that you and your colleagues can work out how the wheel trim ended up on the central reservation, and, eventually, remove it.

6. Look at the vast queues of traffic stretching into the distance and feel tremendously pleased with yourself. You are a powerful and important man. Except that you're not. You are a mealy-mouthed, petty, selfish, ignorant, moustached weasel, you are causing upset, misery and ruination to thousands of strangers, and you look ridiculous in that hat.

HOW **HARD** CAN IT **BE?**

0   5   10

HOW TO... >>>

...DRESS LIKE JEREMY CLARKSON

1. Find a geography teacher.

2. Buy all his clothes off him.

FEEL LIKE A HERO WHILE USING A MICROWAVE OVEN

1. Set the microwave going for the required running time.

2. Momentarily convince yourself that the digital countdown display is not counting down the time until your leftover spag bol will be hot, but is, in fact, connected to a bomb.

3. As the display reaches 0:01, yank the microwave door open.

4. Feel strangely pleased with yourself.

HOW **HARD** CAN IT **BE?**

0   5   10

...DRIVE IN SNOW

(IF YOU ARE A 'MOTORING ORGANISATION')

1. Notice a solitary snowflake drifting past your window.

2. Immediately enter a state of extreme panic.

3. Hurriedly write a press release full of 'winter driving advice' packed with utterly useless cautions, such as 'Don't suddenly mash the brake pedal for no reason',

'Don't deliberately smash your car into a tree' and 'Don't drive unless absolutely necessary' as if the roads of Britain are typically populated by millions of people driving aimlessly round and round in circles for the fun of it.

4. Dispatch one of your representatives to appear on the national news giving yet more fatuous 'advice' as well as the impression that to even look at a car during half an inch of snowfall would result in instant death.

5. Do not actually drive in snow because, according to your own advice, YOU WILL DIE.

...DRIVE IN SNOW
(IF YOU ARE A NORMAL PERSON)

1. Use your judgement.

2. Act like the grown, sentient adult you are.

3. Don't listen to the 'advice' dispensed by motoring organisations.

HOW TO... ≫≫≫

...DRIVE FROM LONDON TO BIRMINGHAM
(THE JAMES MAY METHOD)

1. Consult your *Daily Telegraph Motorists' Atlas* (1957 edition) and memorise a suitable route.

2. Prepare for the impending journey by making a nice cup of tea.

3. Realise that in all the excitement of the tea-making, you have completely forgotten the route.

4. Look up the route again, looking extra hard at all the relevant pages in the *Daily Telegraph Motorists' Atlas* to ensure that the information is retained.

5. Get in to your car and begin your journey, remembering that, although Birmingham is to the north of London, you may not be able to proceed directly north at first, especially if there is a wall in the way.

6. Drive for some considerable time until you see a sign that says 'Welcome to Suffolk'. Realise with some dismay that it has all gone wrong and reset your journey by driving all the way home again and having another cup of tea.

7. Re-consult the *Daily Telegraph Motorists' Atlas* and this time pack some sandwiches.

8. Set off again.

9. Drive for some considerable time until you notice with not inconsiderable disappointment that you can see the sea. Oh dear.

10. Drive around Portsmouth for a bit, then go home.

HOW TO... >>>

...DRIVE FROM LONDON TO BIRMINGHAM

(THE RICHARD HAMMOND METHOD)

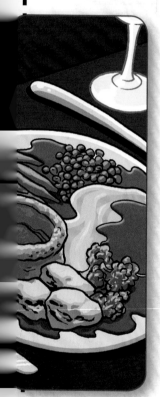

1. Get your sat nav and select the option marked 'home'.

2. Fight through all that nasty London traffic, ooh isn't it busy and nobody has any manners, etc., etc.

3. Drive up the M40 or the M1 until you arrive in Birmingham.

4. Go for a nice carvery dinner. Lovely!

0   5   10

HOW HARD CAN BE

HOW TO... >>>

...DRIVE FROM LONDON TO BIRMINGHAM

(THE JEREMY CLARKSON METHOD)

1. There is literally no way I'm going to Birmingham.

HOW **HARD** CAN IT **BE?**

0   5   10

...BUY TROUSERS

Buying trousers is, without question, the single worst thing a man has to endure.

Firstly, you have to go to the shops, which is unutterably tedious in itself and, contrary to what some might say, no more of a leisure activity than being thrown into a pit and birched.

Secondly, you have to browse clothes when you have almost no opinion about such things and really just want the exact same trousers as you are already wearing but without the frayed bits and that oil stain.

Thirdly, in the act of buying it is generally considered part of the process to try on the trousers which means finding the changing room, going into the little multi-mirrored cubicle, removing your shoes, taking off your existing trousers, putting on the new trousers, removing the new trous... JUST KILL ME NOW.

It doesn't have to be like this, however. Just follow these simple steps for a better trouser-buying experience:

1. Locate a suitable shop, enter the premises and without deviation and hesitation head straight towards the trouser section.

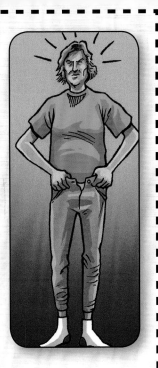

2. Pick the pair of trousers that most closely resembles your existing trousers and in the size that sounds the most familiar.

3. Take the trousers to the till, pay for them and leave the shop as briskly as possible.

4. Next morning, remove the new trousers from the bag and put them on.

5. Discover the new trousers do not fit. Put them back in the bag. Face the shoulder-sagging prospect of having to return to the shop to exchange them for the correct size.

6. Decide to continue wearing your old trousers.

HOW HARD CAN IT BE?

0   5   10

...BUY AN OLD BRITISH SPORTS CAR

1. Does the advert describe it as 'In factory condition'? Do you realise that this means 'Shoddy, wonky and with half of an egg sandwich left inside one of the door panels'?

2. Is one of the things you look for in a car that water stays out and oil stays in? If so, run away now.

3. Do you have a mental image of parping down a country lane on a beautiful summer's day? Does that mental image also contain the bit where you find yourself standing in the country lane next to a stationary car that is spewing out steam and a mysterious green fluid? If no, then, again, run away.

4. If you have not been put off yet, it's time to inspect the car. First question: 'Does it have any rust? If the answer is no,

the second question is, 'How have they
concealed the rust?'

5. Does the hood look like a tramp's hat?
   Good, that's normal.

6. Ask to start the engine. How long

does the current owner have to spend describing to you the very delicate and complicated procedure you must go through in order to get the motor to turn? If it is less than 10 minutes, that's good. If it is more than 10 minutes, that's still completely normal.

7. Blue smoke on start-up can tell you a lot about the condition of the engine. As it fires, look carefully. Can you still see the rest of the car through the smoke cloud? If yes, that's a good sign. If no, that's completely normal. One word of advice – that man approaching through the haze is probably from the Environment Agency.

8. Take a test drive and pay close attention to details such as how many attempts it takes you to get the car into first gear. Less than five is good, but if you are thinking of entering the car in Concours events this may be considered inauthentic. More than 20 attempts is perfectly normal. Take this opportunity to say 'Oh, blast!' a few times as the

gearbox makes an unholy grinding noise. It's worth getting the practice in.

9. Get out on the open road. Be on the lookout for things such as loud knocking noises, unexplained screeching, dangerously vague steering and a sudden bang followed by total loss of drive. These are all completely normal.

10. Have you considered just buying a Mazda MX5?

...RUN A TYRE AND EXHAUST CENTRE

1. Set the tone by equipping your waiting room with a single striplight that is brighter than the sun, five plastic chairs with bits snapped off the sides, a six-year-old copy of *What Car?* magazine with half of the cover ripped off, and a machine that dispenses a tepid fluid that claims to be coffee but more accurately replicates the colour, odour and taste of a turd dipped in chlorine.

2. Top off the threatening atmosphere by giving the impression that you know a lot more about tyres and exhausts than does the customer (even though at least two of your staff are so stupid that they regularly get the two things confused).

3. Listen carefully to the precise size, make and model of tyre that the customer is asking for, wait until he or she has finished and then tell them you do not have it in stock.

4. Claim that the correct tyre is showing up 'on the system' and disappear into a back room to 'ring the Carlisle branch', while actually putting your feet up for 5 minutes to browse through some softcore pornography.

5. Close early.

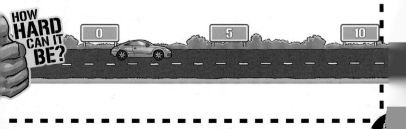

...DEAL WITH POST

In this modern age of email and apps, old-fashioned paper post is a pesky distraction from the more important things in life, like reading emails and downloading apps. Dealing with the steady stream of admin that results from bank statements, renewals notices and junk mail slapping on to your mat doesn't need to be a chore, though, as long as you use this cunning system developed by *Top Gear*'s director of procrastination, Professor James May.

1. Whenever post arrives, DO NOT open it. Simply put it into a pre-designated place and ignore it.

2. Add more post to the pile whenever it comes through the door, until you create a thrillingly perilous Leaning Tower of Post.

3. Wait.

4. Has anyone attempted to repossess your house / demanded money with menaces

/ turned up on the doorstep claiming to be your daughter / set a live wolf on you?

5. If the answer is 'no' (and in all likelihood it will be) then you can be certain that none of the post was important, and you can throw the entire tower away before it falls over and crushes something. Problem solved!

6. Ah, yes, one more thing: If the answer to the above question was in fact 'Yes' and you are now in prison, then ignore all of this in future. Clearly this system is not for you. Sorry.

HOW HARD CAN IT BE?

0   5   10

HOW TO... >>>

...DRESS LIKE RICHARD HAMMOND

1. Find out where Tony Hadley out of Spandau Ballet lives (in the early 1980s).

2. Buy all his clothes off him.

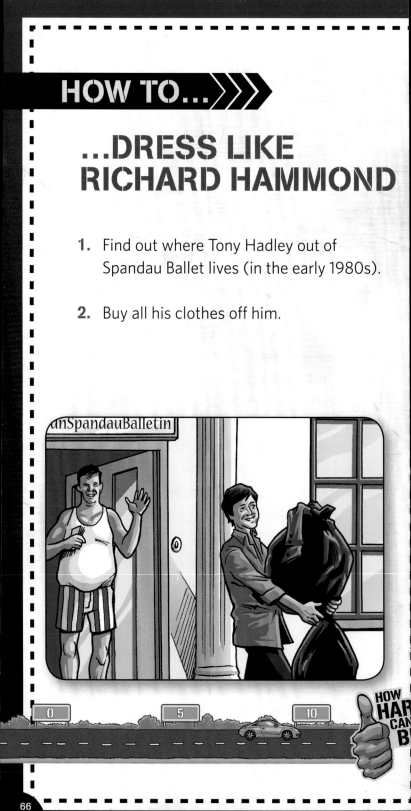

...DRIVE A PEUGEOT

Peugeots have somehow become the worst-driven cars on the road. It is now almost a given that when you encounter a car doing 40mph in the outside lane, it will be a Peugeot. When you find someone causing an entire county to grind to a halt because they can't understand how mini-roundabouts work, they will be in a Peugeot. When you see an accident, you can be sure that the crumpled wreck at its core will be a Peugeot. Unfortunately, the authorities were not interested in Jeremy's idea to station police officers inside Peugeot dealerships to confiscate the driving licence of anyone who stepped inside to buy a car. Instead, we offer the following Peugeot-driving guidance:

1. That pedal on the right. PRESS IT.

2. See above.

3. If you are struggling with points 1 and 2, have you considered taking the bus?

HOW **HARD** CAN IT **BE?**

0   5   10

...DO A HANDBRAKE TURN

1. This is important. It is a little-acknowledged fact that women are deeply impressed by handbrake turns. Yes, yes, they might *pretend* to find them silly and childish, but, as every 19-year-old man knows, that's just a ruse to cover the deep, simmering well of sexual desire that is created the second that a man performs the frankly erotic act of thumbing the button, yanking the handle and feeling the tail come round.

2. So, here we go. Build up a bit of speed.

3. Quickly twist the wheel hard round in the appropriate direction while simultaneously yanking on the handbrake.

4. Wait for the car to come to a halt in the parking spot / hedge / ditch / her father's vegetable garden. Look calmly at your female companion with pride and expectation.

5. Warning: you may now be smothered in kisses by a girl; possibly more than one girl. This probably won't happen immediately. It probably won't happen at all. But, rest assured, this is simply because she is fighting every natural urge in her body and masking her desires by adopting an expression of utter disdain and saying misleading things like, 'What the hell did you do that for? God, just take me home, you pathetic tit!'

6. You may now get out of the car and attempt to locate the missing wheel(s).

HOW HARD CAN IT BE?

0   5   10

...HAVE A PERSONALISED NUMBER PLATE

1. First of all, become moderately vulgar with a misguided sense of how best to spend your disposable income.

2. Develop a strange form of dyslexia in which numbers and crude combinations of numbers appear to you as perfectly normal letters.

3. Buy a number plate that, in your mind, displays your name even though it patently doesn't (unless your name really is G140HAM).

4. Drive around imagining that your car looks more stylish and that you appear more impressive and interesting. DO NOT at any time question why on earth any sensible person would want their own name (or a distant version of it) plastered on to their car. Also, ignore people who insist

on calling you 'J-ELEVEN-NET' or
'D-FOURHUNDREDANDTEN-ID'.

5. Get home one day to discover that,
   because you live in a small town and
   drive an easily identifiable car, the
   burglars have spotted when you're
   elsewhere and casually ransacked your
   house. Ah, now, you didn't think of that
   one, did you?

...*REALLY* HAVE A PERSONALISED NUMBER PLATE

1. Don't.

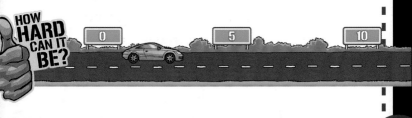

HOW TO... »»

...HAVE A CLASSIC CAR

First of all, let's be clear here. We're not talking about some ultra-rare 1960s Ferrari worth a few billion pounds. In this case, 'classic' almost certainly means an MGB or some other wonky old British car that spends most of its life sitting on your driveway dribbling toxic liquids into the begonias.

1. DO NOT grow a beard.

2. DO NOT refer to your car as 'the old girl'.

3. DO NOT buy a special sort of hat that you only wear when driving it.

4. DO NOT drive hundreds of miles to a classic car show so that you can spend the day wandering about a damp field looking at a load of old cars that are basically exactly the same as yours.

5. DO NOT secretly hope that on any given journey your 'classic' will suddenly

develop a debilitating malfunction
that will give you an excuse to open
the bonnet and have a good old root
around in the engine bay, getting oil
under your fingernails and grease in
your teeth and utterly belying the real

reason that you bought the damn thing, which was so that you could waste half your life endlessly tinkering with it in a vain attempt to make it work properly (despite knowing that this is something even the people who designed and built it signally failed to do).

6. DO NOT expect to be invited to any more dinner parties.

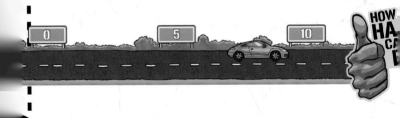

...MAKE A SNOW-PLOUGH OUT OF A COMBINE HARVESTER

1. Find a combine harvester. This should be pretty easy. If it's harvest time it will be listlessly driving up and down a field at about 2mph. If it's not harvest time, it will be uselessly hiding in a shed, the idle swine. But not any longer – because you're about to put it to work in the winter! Oh yes.

2. First, remove the turny thing on the front. It doesn't have a name, it's just the turny thing that normally harvests crops. Do make sure that the combine harvester is yours to muck about with or, at the very least that the farmer who owns it is fine for you to turn it into a snowplough. Trust us, you do not want to anger a farmer. They have shotguns. Replace the turny thing from the front of the combine with a large, custom-made plough.

...MAKE A SNOWPLOUGH OUT OF A COMBINE HARVESTER

3. Turn the big boom thing that dispenses grain into a gravel gun. You might have to wind down the motor a little bit, or it could take someone's eye out.

4. Fit a flame-thrower to the back. This is strictly optional and, on reflection, not an especially good idea for two reasons. Firstly, you might set fire to pedestrians. And secondly, while it's all well and good melting the snow as you pass, it turns out that in very cold weather that melted snow then freezes to leave the road covered in something called 'ice', and that can get very messy indeed.

5. Hey presto, your snowbine is ready to go! Unless, of course, there is no snow. In

which case, your new machine is about
as useful as an actual combine in winter.
Have you considered going to Norway?
They've got loads of snow up there!

HOW TO... >>>

...RUN DOT-MATRIX SIGNS ON MOTORWAYS

1. Have a meeting at which you come up with some fatuous slogans to put on your dot-matrix signs when they're not being used to dispense actual, useful information.

2. If you're stuck, here are some suggestions:
   FOG
   DON'T LITTER
   RAIN IS WET
   DON'T FORGET YOUR CAR!
   TRY NOT TO CRASH!
   DON'T FACE BACKWARDS WHILE
      DRIVING

3. Put your feet up.

HOW
HAR
CAN
B

...*REALLY* RUN DOT-MATRIX SIGNS ON MOTORWAYS

1. Show messages and slogans that might actually have some effect. Here are some examples;
   HURRY UP
   STOP DRIVING LIKE A COCK
   PEUGEOT DRIVERS – INSIDE LANE ONLY

2. Alternatively, if there's nothing of any importance to say, here's a radical thought – just leave the bloody things blank.

...RECEIVE DIRECTIONS FROM A STRANGER

Asking for directions is an absolute last resort to be used only if you are about to miss your own wedding or the birth of your first child. In the event of such an emergency, here is how you must receive them:

1. Uh-huh

2. Yep

3. Yep

4. Uh-huh

5. Left again... okay

6. Okay

7. Yep

8. Right

9. That's great, thanks.

10. Realise you didn't really listen to anything after 'Go to the end of this street we're on now...'

0   5   10

HOW
HAR
CAN
B

...START WHAT YOU'RE SAYING
(IF YOU'RE A *TOP GEAR* PRESENTER)

1. 'Now...'

2. Ah, hang on a minute. 'Now' is a very good way to grab people's attention as you start on a new topic, a sort of verbal new paragraph, if you will, but it's not so good if you're already in the middle of an item and you're doing a voiceover about what your colleagues are up to at a different location. Hang on a sec; let's think of something else.

3. 'Meanwhile...'

HOW **HARD** CAN IT **BE?**

0   5   10

...MAKE A HAM SANDWICH
(THE RICHARD HAMMOND WAY)

1. Get some nice, plain white bread. None of that fancy stuff with bits in it.

2. Open a packet of ham. Not that silly organic stuff that's all odd shapes and has bits of gristle on it. Eww! No, what you want is some nice, processed ham. I know what shape ham should be, and that shape is square. It should also be slightly wet. That shows you it's fresh.

3. Lay out two slices of bread on the worktop and apply a nice layer of lovely supermarket own-brand margarine. DO NOT use butter; it will ruin your sandwich by making it taste all buttery.

4. Before applying the moist, wafer-thin square of ham, scan the surrounding area for poisonous interlopers such as lettuce, tomato and other natural dangers that can infiltrate a ham sandwich, making it completely inedible.

5. Once you are completely confident that nothing is going to contaminate your sandwich, press the square of ham on to one slice of bread, apply the other slice of bread to the top and slice straight down the middle, leaving two rectangles.

6. Drive to the Lake District, climb up a mountain, sit in the drizzle and eat. Yummy!

...DESIGN A SAAB

1. Lock yourself in a room full of pictures of aeroplanes.

2. After two weeks, leave the room full of pictures of aeroplanes and design a car that looks nothing like an aeroplane because, as it turns out, cars and aeroplanes are quite different, and trying to pretend that one is inspired by the other is a load of old cobblers.

3. Make sure your car has some quite good ideas in it, but looks slightly odd.

4. Confirm how slightly odd it is by putting some of the controls in places you wouldn't expect. For example, the ignition on the floor. Or the switch that controls the windscreen wipers on top of the headrest.

5. Sit back and wait for customers to arrive. You will be able to spot them because they will be either architects or graphic designers, and will be wearing black

rollneck sweaters or some exquisitely thin and arty spectacles. Possibly simultaneously.

6. Realise that, unfortunately, there aren't enough car-loving architects and graphic designers in the world to sustain your business. Go bust.

...BE A
MOTORCYCLIST
(ACCORDING TO JEREMY CLARKSON)

1. Buy a leather romper suit because you like leather and that's basically the whole reason you got a motorcycle in the first place.

2. Arrange to meet up with some other men in leather and 'go for a ride', which is motorcycling code for 'zoom about the countryside making lots of unnecessary noise while staring lustfully at the leather-clad bottom of the man in front'.

3. Stop at a country pub so you can all stand around outside sipping bitter lemon, admiring each other's leather clothes and talking almost entirely in meaningless letters and numbers.

4. Set off again. Get so distracted by the leather-clad bottom of the man in front that you veer off the road and hit a tree, which does at least mean that someone else can have your eyes and kidneys.

The views of Jeremy Clarkson are not those
of other members of the *Top Gear* team.
For example, Richard Hammond and James
May, both of whom like motorbikes and
think Jeremy is an idiot.

...MAKE A SMOOTHIE

Smoothies are all well and good but they always contain needless 'healthy' items like mung beans, seeds and moss. In consultation with *Top Gear*'s chief health-and-well-being scientist, Dr Jeremy Clarkson, we've come up with a far more manly smoothie, as follows.

1. First, you will need a food blender. And not one of those weedy ones that works on electricity. Yours needs to be connected to a V8 engine. We have favoured a 6.2-litre General Motors LS3, but any small-block, high-displacement unit would do.

2. With your V8 hooked up to your blender, it's time to add your ingredients. Don't worry about gently stirring them in one by one. Just dump the whole lot in together from the off.

Hunks of beef
Bovril
Worcestershire sauce
Tabasco sauce

Chillies
Bricks
Nails
Castrol GTX

3. Blend the ingredients until the clanking and grinding noises subside. Or get louder. Either is fine. If bits start flying off you might need to switch off the V8 while you assess the damage to furniture, windows and load-bearing parts of your house.

4. Mop up any spillage.

5. Pour a serving of smoothie into a glass and drink in one.

6. Mop up any vomit.

7. Go to hospital.

...BE A FORMULA 1 DRIVER

1. Buy a sort of grown-up's romper suit and plaster it with the names of at least half-a-dozen companies, some of which

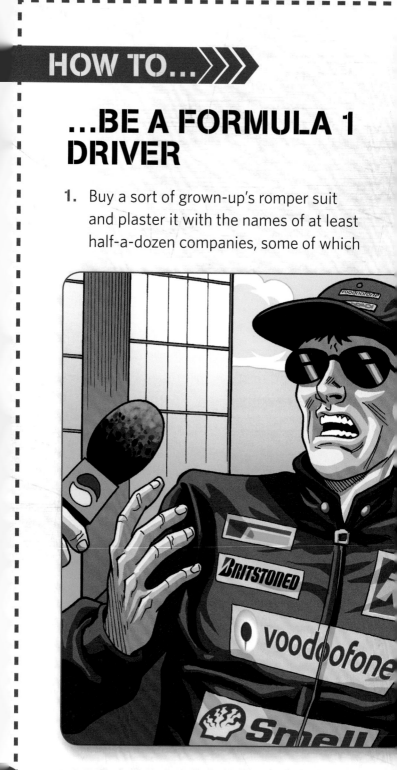

you have heard of; some of which you have never seen before in your life, and which turn out to do faintly inexplicable but extremely lucrative things like selling money to banks.

2. Wear a cap that matches your overalls, and which becomes such a permanent fixture on your head whenever you're not

wearing a crash helmet that it would be reasonable to assume that you sleep and shower in it.

3. Whenever you're not actually driving a racing car remember to put on a rather ghastly watch, also made by one of your sponsors, and so horrendously over-sized that it makes it hard to lift your wrist above waist level without help.

4. Wear a pair of conspicuously branded sunglasses that are so unfashionable that, to the untrained observer, they may have been stolen off someone's grandmother during the 1970s.

5. Use your substantial pay cheques to a) attract a sensationally attractive girlfriend and b) buy a private jet. Use the latter to take the former to your yacht for the weekend. Still manage to look a bit miserable.

6. Constantly refer to your team as 'the guys' and repeatedly insist that they have 'done a great job'.

7. Moan that your car isn't working properly.

8. Moan about another driver.

9. Give television interviews in which you convey a sense that your exciting, glamorous, jet-setting international lifestyle is in fact an enormous chore, and that if you worked in an abattoir you would perhaps be far less of a grumpy bastard.

BE A FORMULA 1 DRIVER
(THE KIMI RÄIKKÖNEN METHOD)

1. Ignore as much of the previous page as possible.

2. Drive fast.

3. Swear.

4. Get drunk.

5. Mumble.

...MAKE A CHINESE CAR

1. To get you started, buy some old bits off Fiat or similar. Failing that, buy an actual Toyota or Honda and just copy it.

2. Design a new bodyshell, remembering that ideally it must look a bit like lots of other cars but also be as bland as a glass of tepid water served from a beige beaker.

3. Come up with an equally plain design for the interior. Remember, when choosing

Nissan Micra

Wistful Tiger

the type of plastic for the dashboard, your watchwords should be 'thin' and 'sweaty'.

4. Give your car a name that sounds faintly comical to visiting Westerners such as 'Smooth Wolf', 'Wistful Tiger' or 'Hot Bassoon 88'.

5. Ignore the jocular remarks of European idiots, quietly continue to practise car making and slowly destroy them all.

HOW HARD CAN IT BE?

0   5   10

...BUY FLOWERS

Buying flowers is generally quite easy if you are a woman. If you are a man, however, it is not. This guide should help.

1. First, check that you are NOT in a petrol station. Petrol stations are fine places from which to buy petrol, screen wash and slightly damp logs. They are not a good place from which to buy flowers, and presenting a lady with a bunch of wilting, grim-covered, floppy stems in a crinkly plastic cone is tantamount to presenting her with a bouquet of roast dog turds.

2. Consider going to an actual florist's shop. But beware. An actual florist's shop is going to be staffed by actual florists, and actual florists are going to ask you awkward questions such as 'What sort of flowers does she like?' and 'How much are you looking to spend?', neither of which you are equipped to answer without fear of seeming inattentive and/ or tight-fisted. Think carefully before

you pursue this option, lest you come away having spent £60 on three sprigs of green stuff with a vast yellow triffid in the middle, which you then accidentally shut in the car door on the way home.

3. For a safe middle ground, try a decent sort of supermarket, which will most likely stock some flowers that are still clinging to life and which you can browse without fear of interrogation.

4. Browse the flowers.

5. Realise that you have literally no interest in, or opinion on, flowers.

6. Just buy the brightest-looking, most expensive bunch.

7. Realise that they still only cost a tenner.

8. Consider going back and buying a second identical bunch to look more generous. Decide one bunch appears lavish enough, and she will never know how much they cost anyway.

9. Present flowers to loved one with much flourish.

10. Realise that you forgot to peel off the price label.

...MAKE A CAR-BASED MOTORHOME

1. Buy an old Lotus Excel and, using aviation technology (from the 1920s), create an aerodynamic pod that fits on to the roof and contains everything that you need. As long as things you need do not include 'a good night's sleep', 'a place to do any half-decent cooking' or 'a proper lavatory' or... actually, on reflection, this is a terrible idea. We've had another thought...

2. Buy an old Land-Rover and fill the back with an elaborate series of panels that will fold out to make an entire house, capable of being assembled in less than four days, and providing warmth and security in anything up to a very, very light breeze and... actually, this is an even worse idea. Sorry, start again...

3. Buy an old Citroën CX estate and build on top of it a modernist, *Grand Designs-*

style tower block that will in no way utterly compromise the ride, handling and road-holding of the vehicle beneath, so that what was once a perfectly acceptable family car is now a mobile death trap that wobbles every time someone looks at it, causing... sorry, sorry, sorry, this is literally the worst idea in the world.

4. Check in to a hotel.

HOW
HAR
CAN
BE

...NOT BE ABLE TO RELAX AFTER READING THIS PAGE

1. Are you sure you locked the car?

HOW **HARD** CAN IT **BE?**

...MAKE A HAM SANDWICH

(THE JAMES MAY WAY)

1. Carefully remove two slices of bread from their packaging.

2. Lay out the bread slices adjacent to each other in the designated sandwich-construction area of your kitchen. Using Dymo tape or small cards, label the slices 'Bread slice 1' and 'Bread slice 2'.

3. Using a thick-bladed domestic knife, apply butter to each slice of bread at a quantity of 0.45g per square inch.

4. Remove the ham from the appropriately-labelled ham section of the fridge.

5. Carefully measure one of the bread slices using your sandwich-measuring tape (don't worry about the other slice; if taken from the same cross section of loaf they should be broadly the same, +/- 1mm). Note down the dimensions in your notebook marked 'Sandwich-making (various)'.

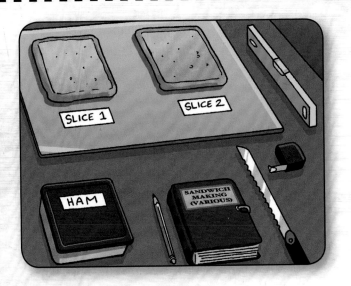

6. Now measure the ham and trim accordingly to the same precise dimensions as the bread using a thin-bladed, rubber-handled 110mm kitchen knife. Remember to wash the knife thoroughly after use and replace it in the correct place on the wall, as designated by the matching outline and/or label.

7. Using both hands for a steady grip, carefully lay the dimensionally accurate ham precisely upon bread slice 1. If necessary, adjust the ham in the north-south, east-west planes and rotationally until it sits in perfect alignment with the bread underneath.

8. Take bread slice 2 and lower it carefully on to the bread slice 1 and ham beneath.

...MAKE A HAM SANDWICH
(THE JAMES MAY WAY)

Again, make adjustments where necessary until alignment is correct.

9. Remove your sandwich-making spirit level and plumb line from their allotted storage places and check that all sides of the sandwich are aligned and straight.

10. Take the 160mm kitchen knife from the 'medium-to-large' section of the knife-storage rack and remove your sandwich protractor from its protective sheath.

11. Use the sandwich protractor to measure the perfect 45° line across the sandwich. Measure at least twice to avoid error.

12. Use the 160mm knife to cut the sandwich into two halves, along the pre-measured 45° line.

13. Now go to the cupboard marked 'Plates (<22cm)'...

(continued pages 132 – 243)

HOW
HAR
CAN
BE

0   5   10

HOW TO... >>>

...SPEND THE REST OF THE DAY WONDERING WHERE IT IS YOU'VE SEEN THESE WORDS BEFORE

1. Sicursiv

2. Angram

3. Grohe

Sorry.

...DESIGN THE PORSCHE 911

1. Come up with a new sports car with a slanted back and the engine in the wrong place.

2. Go on holiday for a few years.

3. Eventually return from holiday. Get original plans for the sports car. Colour in the bumpers. Go on holiday again.

4. Some years later, return from holiday. Dig out original plans for the sports car. Get some marker pens and draw new bumpers over the top. Book a cruise.

5. Return from your extended cruise. Find plans for the original sports car. Rub out the headlights. Draw them again, a little bit differently. Hear that Mauritius is nice at this time of year.

6. Get back from your lengthy holiday. Fetch plans for the original sports car. Stick on photocopier. Enlarge to 105 per

cent. Consider buying holiday home in Tuscany.

7. Pop into the office on the way back from your new house in Tuscany. Pull original sports-car plans out of the drawer, cut down the middle, stretch slightly, head back to the pool.

8. It seems to have worked so far. Repeat for the next 50 years.

0   5   10

...FIGHT CRIMES (IN THE 1970s)

1. Buy a Jensen Interceptor.

2. Zoom about a bit in an exuberant and stylish manner, powersliding across runways, crashing through cardboard boxes and so on.

3. Pull up to a fancy London club and walk straight in because they know you.

4. Punch a man in a fez.

5. Zoom about a bit more with some pretty girls in the back seat.

6. Repeatedly machine gun a baddie, but make sure that no actual blood comes out.

7. Go home for a period of quiet reflection in which you pin some rare butterflies into a frame or assemble a ship in a bottle.

8. Receive some startling news on a red telephone.

9. Zoom around a mountain road (which looks strangely unrealistic in the interior shots).

10. Spot the baddie disappearing into an underground station.

11. Let the baddie see you are on to him and pursue him through the station, inexplicably closing in on him even though he is doing a panicky run and you are only maintaining a brisk walk.

12. Karate chop the man in the neck so that he falls to the ground. Retrieve the bomb / diamonds / top secret plans from the man's briefcase.

13. Return to your Interceptor. Pause to stare into the middle distance with a steely gaze.

14. Call the AA because the bloody Interceptor won't start again.

HOW HARD CAN IT BE?

0   5   10

...BUILD A CARAVAN AIRSHIP

1. Find a suitable hangar in which to build your airship. *Top Gear* used Cardington, but any vast inter-war, airship-specific structure will do.

2. Do some sums on the back of a laptop. Realise that this is more complicated than it first seemed and decide to switch on the laptop.

3. Oh, cock! The laptop has melted under the sheer complexity of the sums. Get a

bigger computer. Do some even bigger maths.

4. Finally, use all the results of the maths to commission a purpose-built airship envelope.

5. Oh, cock! Discover that, despite the purpose-built airship envelope, the caravan is still too heavy.

6. Lighten the caravan by throwing away all the unnecessary stuff like cushions, ornamental plates, horse brasses and so on. Re-build the kitchenette out of lightweight airplane materials. Consider commissioning a titanium khazi.

7. Inflate envelope. Prepare for maiden flight.

8. Oh, cock! It's too windy. Go home again.

9. The weather conditions are perfect. Receive clearance for take-off. Soar majestically into the clear blue skies.

10. Oh, cock! Drift helplessly across the English countryside, inadvertently cross restricted airspace, start losing height, crash into a hedge. Oh, cock! again.

...ANNOY THE PEOPLE OF MEXICO

1. Do NOT annoy the people of Mexico.
    Yes, Richard Hammond, that includes
    you.

HOW
HARD
CAN IT
BE?

0   5   10

HOW TO... 〉〉〉

...PLAY RUGBY WITH CARS

1. Assemble your 'players'. *Top Gear* used the Kia Cee-apostrophe-d for the backs, but any medium-sized hatchback will probably do just as well. For the forwards, get some beefier 4x4s. A Hummer might be overkill unless you are attempting to recreate a classic All Blacks squad, in which case Jonah Lomu must be represented by a lorry.

2. Find a suitable venue. *Top Gear* used Twickenham, but any iconic national stadium will do. You might want to warn them that their grass is going to get a bit scuffed up.

3. Play rugby. No, really. Just go ahead and play rugby. As *Top Gear* proved, it really is possible. Obviously the whole passing-the-ball-backwards rule has to go out of the window, but everything else – scrums, tries, conversions – is entirely possible in a car.

4. Use the knowledge that you have gathered and apply it to other sports. Think about it: the Americans love to wear protective clothing for sports anyway.

They put on helmets to play rounders, for heaven's sake. So let's go the whole hog and play all sports in cars. The marathon would be easy. The 100m would be brilliant. Diving would be SPECTACULAR! Just remember to wind down the window to do the shot-put. And maybe get some little ramps for the hurdles. With those small matters taken care of, it's hard to think of a single sport that couldn't be massively improved if it were played with cars.

5. There we go, then: SPORT SOLVED.

...APPROACH THE STIG

If you're lucky enough to see The Stig out in public, the immediate temptation may be to approach him, perhaps to ask for an autograph, or to pose for a photo. Be warned: this is a VERY dangerous thing to do. For starters, The Stig does not sign autographs but he does like the taste of biro ink, so that's never going to end well. Secondly, he causes a strange glitch in many popular types of digital camera that wipes all photographs from the memory

and replaces them with a single portrait of the actor David Suchet. As such, we would strongly advise against approaching The Stig. If, however, you are determined to do so, perhaps because you'd like what's left of your trousers back, here are a few tips.

1. Locate The Stig and move very slowly towards him from the left side only. DO NOT approach from the right unless you like waking up in Ipswich.

2. Listen carefully. Is The Stig emitting a low humming noise? That's perfectly normal. If there is no humming or the humming is accompanied by a rapid high-pitched noise like an angry glockenspiel, move slowly away from the

area. No, really, we mean this literally. You must immediately move house. Bad things are going to happen.

3. Stop. Do you think The Stig has noticed you? Remember, his vision is based on smell. If you do not think The Stig has noticed you, clap your hands firmly together once. It is vital to alert him to your presence. The Stig sometimes sleeps standing up, and you do not want to wake him suddenly. That's how people lose a finger.

4. If at this stage The Stig runs off, DO NOT chase after him. He will only lead you to a dark place. Or Reading. It depends what his plans are that weekend.

5. If The Stig charges towards you, run away in a zigzag, lifting your knees as high as possible. This will not confuse him; it's to provide additional amusement for onlookers. While being chased by The Stig, the best way to safety is to climb a tree, as if being chased by a brown bear. No, wait, a black

bear. Which bear is it that can't climb trees? Whichever it is, pretend you're escaping from one of those. Although, of course, The Stig can also climb trees, now we think about it.

6. Assuming The Stig has not run away, or run at you, approach him with smooth, slow movements and say in a loud, confident voice, 'Stig! Please return my family!'

7. After that, you're on your own. And let's hope you've remembered to bring a change of clothes.

It's worth remembering that much of the above advice also applies to approaching Richard Hammond.

HOW TO... >>>

...EXIST BY SHOPPING ONLY AT A PETROL STATION

1. **Eating**

   This is a piece of cake, possibly literally. The modern petrol station has everything you need to survive, particularly if you're prepared to be fairly ingenious. The basics are certainly taken care of. They have crisps; they have biscuits; they have pies. Doctors go on all the time about your 'five a day' but you can easily achieve this by buying a large bottle of orange juice and drinking the lot. For fancier dining, get creative by, for example, using watered-down tomato ketchup as a 'jus' and crushing up Quavers to create a 'cheese-crust layer' on slices of corned beef. It's all about lateral thinking (and being prepared to count Super Noodles as a vegetable).

2. **Home furnishings and decor**

   This is entirely achievable, especially since many petrol stations sell plastic garden furniture, and maybe even sun loungers in the summer. Failing that, you could buy a couple of bags of logs and fashion a rudimentary chair from those. Many garages also sell toy cars so

that's ornaments taken care of, or simply buy a few cans of soup, pop them on the mantelpiece and claim it's a knowing reference to Andy Warhol (also, you can open and eat them if it's cold out and you can't be arsed to walk to the petrol station). Pictures are the easiest of the lot: just buy a load of magazines, tear out some pages with nice pictures on them and hang them up. You never know, one of the magazines might even come with a free poster – ideal for those larger walls!

3. **Clothes**

Ah, now, this is a bit trickier. You could try fashioning a shirt out of chamois leathers and those yellow screen dusters, but you might need a sewing machine, and they definitely don't sell those at petrol stations.

Also, you're a bloke who is trying to live on things that he can buy from his local garage. How likely is it that you know how to use a sewing machine, eh? Still, on the bright side, the one piece of 'clothing' you'll never be short of is cheap, blue rubber gloves.

4. **Presents**

Your friends will quickly become used to receiving birthday gifts such as an in-car air freshener, a bottle of screen-wash or a can of frankfurters 'n' beans, all wrapped in old newspaper or crammed inside a cheap, blue rubber glove. Anyone who complains about this isn't worth bothering with. They're clearly the kind of idiot who wastes their life going to actual shops and buying actual things.

5. **Petrol**

You will have absolutely no problems on that front.

0   5   10

HOW
HAR
CAN
B

...PARACHUTE INTO A MOVING CAR

1. Wait, wait, wait. You want to know how to *parachute into a moving car*?

2. Seriously?

3. OK, fine. First of all, are you a parachutist? Please remember that 'parachutist' means something very different to 'man who has a parachute that he bought on a whim from a car boot sale'.

4. Right, now there are several important things to bear in mind here. First of all, you'll need a nice clear day, of course. Secondly, the car must be a convertible. It sounds obvious, but it's amazing how easy it is to forget these things until you're ruefully bouncing off the roof of a Land-Rover Discovery. Thirdly, it helps if the car has a big engine so that the driver can make quick, accurate speed adjustments as you come in to land.

Speaking of which, your approach should be as slow and controlled as possible and, contrary to what you might think, it's best to come in at a shallow angle rather than attempting to drop straight in from above...

5. Are you even taking any of this in? You're not, are you? Fine. One final piece of advice:

6. DO NOT under any circumstances attempt to parachute into a moving car.

HOW HAR CAN B